SOFT WHISPERINGS

A Collection of Short Poems

SOMYA JAIN

ISBN 978-93-5559-194-4

Published in India 2022 by Pencil

A brand of
One Point Six Technologies Pvt. Ltd.
123, Building J2, Shram Seva Premises,
Wadala Truck Terminal, Wadala (E)
Mumbai 400037, Maharashtra, INDIA
E connect@thepencilapp.com
W www.thepencilapp.com

Author biography

Somya is a storyteller and a poetess. Her poems express human feelings and emotions that are gentle, evocative, and thoughtful. Inspired by the beauty of emotions, she loves to add new colors not only to her poems but also her art. As an artist, she loves to explore new realms with colors and to add meaning to the otherwise blank canvases. Her artwork often includes abstract art and figurative art.

When Somya is not writing or painting, she offers consulting services to the corporate clients and is happy to create an impact in the society through her work.

CONTENTS

FROM THE POETESS'S DESK

It is a truth universally acknowledged that a single lady in possession of a good heart must be in want of a book.

It took me more than a hundred poems and verse fragments by Tagore, Dickinson, and Bronte Sisters to finally muster the courage to experience the world from my heart. Women are often labelled as soft, tender, sensitive, emotional, and weak-hearted. While women may govern the world with their feelings, they are often mocked and not taken seriously most times due to the unconscious gender bias.

Soft Whisperings is an initiative to break the barriers that surround women, and the author encourages her readers of all genders to own their emotions, govern their feelings, channel their energy into positive things, and listen to their heart.

This book includes short poems that deal with themes of love, maturity, and courage. Feelings and emotions are woven in strands that reflect the beauty of life and savor moments that are simple yet magical.

TO MY PARENTS

I would like to dedicate this book to my parents.

AUTHOR'S RIGHTS

LOVE

FRAGRANCE OF LOVE

Mysteries of attraction need no logic,

Being each other's sail, together they create magic!

She is his light, his endless desire.

He is her heart, her wild attire.

Her fragrance is poised in every corner of their house,

The mild euphoria is always aroused.

The caterpillar is turning into a butterfly,

Her lush is akin the feeble rays of sunlight that streak the sky.

Love kindles a blush, roseate hue, and coyness anew.

While all around repose, the fragrance from the rose arose.

They don't know how to be husband and wife,

As lovers, together they thrive.

THE VOWS

Unknowingly, he held her hand for the first time,

Little did he know, she was swayed for lifetime.

The intimacy of her smile,

Sends a chill down his spine.

Possessing a temperament of equanimity,

They vow their marriage to be a blend of magic and reality.

Not every love story deserves a sonnet,

Thiers is like spotting a comet.

Exchanging the sweet glares,

And caressing the changing winds,

As they kiss each other with vivacity,

Why they met is no longer a mystery.

Flared, she fills herself with good laughter,

As she reads past her old chapters.

Clearly confusing, constantly changing,

A fine mess, no doubt,

The answer to her question – “Does he remember this as I remember?” – is an open secret.

THE LADY

With a million beats thrilling to dance,

She uncages a thousand thoughts upon the chance.

In every scent of the spring,

She blooms with an essence of a different green.

With an ineluctable passion for her loved ones,

She enlivens sensations of many a dainty heart.

Attired in a rich array,

She crowns the world in every role that she plays.

MAGICAL FIRST MOMENTS

Blushing through the mist and dew,

The mother's life tastes anew.

Like daisies rose-scented,

The father wraps his little one, his present.

The ecstasy of enjoying first moments gleams a bright hue,

Of a magical feeling that the parents never knew.

Hearing melodies soft and sweet,

The child's cry sweeps them off their feet.

Kisses of reverence fill their evening,

As they become the beat of a heart belonging to an infant world.

THE SHOWER OF GRACE

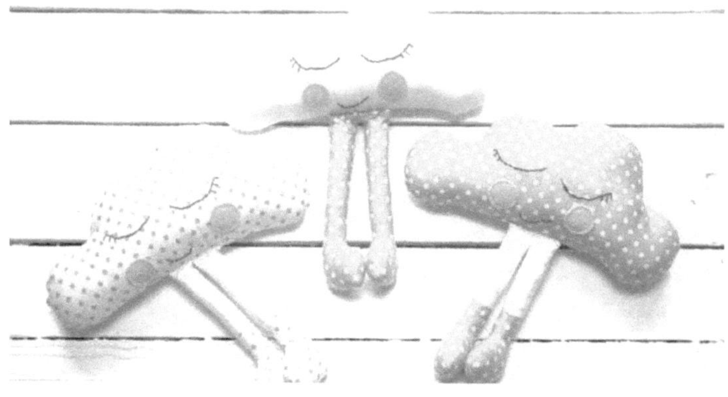

With smiles abound, the child laughs aloud.

Giving warm looks, akin the sun playing with the clouds.

Unaffected by the world, the new born sleeps deep.

The rhythm of the universe moves his light feet.

The crawling child wakes up each morning in pyjamas of bright hue, spellbound,

Rekindling joy and fun in the life of all around.

The shower of grace pumps his happy heart,

The zillion beats dance to the melodious tunes in a cheerful boulevard.

A SOFT RUSTLE

The mug asked the paint tubes,

"How d'you all do this morning?"

And came the greeting,

"As the dew of little things find joy in morning,

We give birth to life each time we are popped up for shining!"

The paint book couldn't resist blowing its hue at the mat,

The mat meanwhile performed poses to stretch its back.

The planters on the shelves were oozing with fragrance,

The smooth notebook pages kept playing with each other in reverence.

"Stay Calm!" whispered the beautiful linen to the comfy cushions,

As the wobbly coffee hugged its cousin, the pretty dress, with fascination!

THE SPINE

Upbeat with a beatitude smile on your face,

You are as serene as flowers in a vase.

As strangers we started our journey,

Now sharing moments that spark jollity.

My thoughts swirl, you lend me your advice,

Together we admire the picturesque paradise.

We swing from one strand to another,

You are my spine, my jewel, my fire.

THE SACRED BODY

The body is where our soul lives,

The body is sacred.

Every touch arouses sweet sensations,

Every atom breathes fire, embracing perfection.

The body resembles purity,

Adorning nothing but fine curves and smiles.

Titillating all senses,

The body resides in a free flowing Goddess.

BLISS

What a poet seeks is an essence in reality,

His atoms are the fragments of entirety.

Poems of heart decorate the pages of his diary,

Blooming flowers of all colors teach him the meaning of purity.

He may be afraid of the pause in continuity,

But in this very pause, he talks beautifully.

While sipping the sacred tea, suddenly he is awakened,

With the vibrant colors slowly melting within, he forgets his errand.

He swings upon finding his recipe of bliss,

And rejoices in the sonorous sounds dancing on his lips.

This, dear readers, is the story of every kiss.

STRANGERS

He walked up to her in a crowded room,

Letting their friendship bloom.

She waved and they exchanged more than just a glare,

Enjoying the dizzy dreams of an unknown sphere.

A fateful meeting for the blushing souls,

Unfolded the unending desire to hide the truth.

In sweet glances, good laughter, and idiotic fun,

Riding the waves of chance,

The strangers soon became one.

A PHONE CALL

So difficult it is to be alone,

To not have your friend give you a phone.

The one to whom you let out your secret,

Bursting all emotions with the speed of a rocket.

You keep telling your heart to stay strong,

While going weak all day long.

You keep waiting endlessly for that one call,

From your friend,

Who lifts you up every time you fall.

ON LOVE - A NOTE FOR MY READERS

Whether it is our witty Emma Woodhouse acknowledging that there is no charm equal to tenderness of heart or the sensible Marianne Dashwood who had convinced herself to never see a man whom she could really love as she required so much, we, the caretakers of our delicate heart, often find ourselves tangled in many a emotion.

Trust me when I tell you that the very lines which you are reading with an impenetrable calmness hold the power to drive the lovers wild.

Seeing a butterfly

Before the date night

Makes me high

Meeting after long

Savoring each moment, day-long

To each other we belong

The story of my song

Makes me weak when I want to be strong

For many such magical nights, I long

XOXO

COMING OF AGE

MOMENT OF EPIPHANY

Uncertainty gives birth to destiny,

Destiny leaps up to a new story.

My moment of epiphany kindles faith,

When many a thing are barefaced.

How long does hope live I ask,

To hope when everything becomes unsurmountable becomes a task.

Of all the deeds I commit in my life,

The craziest is to stop believing in life.

I saw a comet one starry night,

Now I gaze at the sky, each night with delight.

I may walk down many an empty road,

But I am at home in my quiet memory road.

Moments may happen for a moment in epiphany,

And it takes eternity to understand their moonlight simplicity.

I see life reveal its meaning,

Slowly as the universe energy is healing.

THE BLOOM OF YOUTH

Tiptoeing from childhood to adulthood,

I blossom like a lotus of many petals.

Appreciating flaws like inconstancy of seasons,

I rejoice like angels dancing in the heaven.

Soft singing, I am the sonorous beauty,

In communion with the Almighty.

I balance myself like the pillars of temple,

The dew of little things give strength to the heart, that's a little feeble.

Words flow freely in my book of pictures,

As I adorn love, my haute couture.

THE MORPHOSIS

With the heart of a girl and the charm of a woman,

She tried getting upon the world by just a smile.

Protecting her jovial heart, one that only spread love,

The heart had to pass several tests of betrayal and of wrath.

They tried changing her so she would turn into one of those ugly,

Little did they know, they were playing with the fire of the holy.

Fighting demons in her mind wasn't easy,

Why should she be her own enemy, do you not agree?

In the wild world where each day is a battle,

Easy to give up, but she continues to show her mettle.

Even when things turn bad out there,

This little girl doesn't forget to take good care.

Breaking her heart was easy,

But breaking her will not be wheezy.

INDIVIDUALITY

We seek individuality,

When all we want is similarity.

Always appreciating perfection,

We forget to embrace our imperfection.

Constantly pressing buttons when stuck,

We get burst by an pin and call it luck.

Believing in happily ever-after,

When are we happy ever?

We are afraid of reaching heights,

Yet we delight upon seeing a meteorite.

Not becoming a wallflower who understands yet remains quiet,

Let's step into the wild world,

Without regret, with all our might.

NOSTALGIA

You are an epitome of grace and kindness,

I always look forward to your guidance.

Without you, I am spineless,

You are my life's brightness.

A man of good heart

For all my problems, you have a dart.

Oh! My Santa Claus,

Moments spent with you are filled with awes,

You have been brooming away my flaws,

From the day I first crawled.

THE HOP

Flying so high that vultures fly low,

We stir the silent air, in the sun and in snow.

Without ever feeling the forest canopy,

We run wild, only to drop to the knee.

Sitting on the seat that's for sitting,

We care for things that do nothing.

It's time now to hop like a pecan, bloom like an orchid,

Together, let's blossom in a world, where the "us" is no longer meaner.

GROWING UP - A NOTE FOR MY READERS

Do we ever really grow up? While we may behave like rational adults, deep down we are still that child who wants to live in their own world without worrying about having to step into the wild world ever...

Bed of roses

Or a garden of all flowers and shrubs

Life as we know it, is often messed up

Dress up, glam up

On days when you don't feel like getting up

Grab your coffee and look at your book telling you "pick me up"

XOXO

COURAGE

FEAR

Kill it before it kills you,

Crawl out of the void before it eats you.

You think the worst will happen to you,

But know that everything you think will not be true.

Fighting the demons in your mind isn't easy,

Why be your own enemy; don't you agree?

It's a wild world and each day is a battle,

Easy to give up, but for once, can u show them your mettle?

Break the rusted chains of your friendship with stress,

And get comfortable with your mess.

Change, the only constant, will soon dispel your haze,

Choosing faith over fear will help you to get out of your maze.

SHE IS FORGIVING

A Frail spirit, a feeble heart,

Bend like an oak before the mighty fault.

The tedious hours of waiting,

Swirl into a reverie.

For enticing moments of baiting,

Tiptoe from expectations to reality.

Soon after the joy of little things,

Break forth myriad tunes within,

Strength gives birth to utterance ineffable,

For the ardent hope is also forgiving.

THE PHOENIX

Life swung by fast,

Realization dawned upon her at last,

The universe became a paradox,

She felt trapped in her hoax.

The shadow followed her perpetually,

Blooming love and hate, synchronously.

Rusted by the chains of her thought,

Emotions that she longer wrought,

The chimera untied her last knot,

And took the shot with all haught.

DIFFERENT FROM YOU

I zone myself out of life's default,

Life's a riddle, not perfect but flawed.

Songs unsung, poems unheard

I uncover a many story hidden in my world.

I am impatient as the wait makes me tired,

Crawling, I finally come out of the void.

I am fearless and a spicy mess,

Realize this as I caress my tress.

Whatever I do, I do it for love,

I am not weak, I am not strong,

A little different from you and that's all!!

BE HIS PRIDE

If he smiles a smile,

Know that he may have cried last night.

He looks up to you to cheer him up,

A few minutes of your time can save his world.

He has been through a lot, he feels,

Life drives him crazy, but he finds peace when asleep.

Wake up, talk to him, be with him,

He may not say it, but you will know it.

When the world gives up on him,

Hope comes to lift him up.

Ignore him, mock him, leave him alone,

He won't complain and still hope to be with you again.

A step is better than no step.

So, do your bit, save a life,

Give up your ego, be his pride.

FIND YOURSELF - A NOTE FOR MY READERS

"Stay Strong" - Yes, easier said than done. We have all been in situations where we lost a part of ourselves either by choice or by force. Do we really need time to remind us to find our lost selves?

My treasure hunt begins

On delicate strands I swing

All seasons feel like spring

I grow up

Forget my ice-cream truck

Believing that it's my luck

XOXO

BEAUTY OF LIFE

THE WHISTLING TRAILS

My heart's happiness enlivens sensations,

Enough to get to the meaning of poems;

Radiating richness in an embrace,

It satisfies all urges of pleasure and of leisure.

The myriad tastes of life awaken me,

The songs of spring rouse the busy bee,

The oozing fragrance of rose leaves many a whistling trail,

The evening becomes pleasing in this delightful tale.

Sipping the showering nectar, I mediate calmly;

Unwinding all strings, I explore the realm of chemistry!

THE PERFECT GETAWAY

Looking toward the ocean with delight,

I walk by the shore upright.

When my feet touch the beach sand,

The waves start flowing like mad.

I am drifted from mundanity,

I am lifted from insanity.

Pacing myself, I sit on the sea sand,

As the sky goes la la land.

With the gentle kiss of the wind, passion kicks in,

The pristine water ripples send my heart into a spin.

Wrapping serenity in my arms, sun swept,

Daintily I catch up with my heart!!!

THE WISH

Oh! ball of mirth,

How I wish I were like you,

Unaffected by the world,

I groove to tunes unheard,

As beautiful dreams all come true.

Oh! the color of feelings,

I dance as you twirl and swirl,

And how I wish I could choose you,

As I paint my mind in a bright hue.

Oh! bubble of satisfaction,

How I wish I could hold you,

At home in my heart,

And joy in my cart,

To all my worries, I ah choo!

THE WEEKEND

Fun Friday begins

Excitement begins to build up

With each passing hour

Saturday finally arrives

A joyful palette of colors brightens the mood

With fluting sounds abound

A warm Sunday afternoon

Paves way for anxiety

As Monday is near

THE LOCKDOWN HOLIDAY

I blissfully sip my coffee,

Wondering akin unwrapping a toffee.

Sumptuous food sets good mood,

Followed by a bath, surely feels good.

A new chapter starts, one that is only mine,

Of course, without any sorry this time,

Like a plane taxing on the runway,

I'll now unwind and enjoy my confetti day!!!

THE COLORS OF JOY

Tender red showers its nectar on pink,

Meanwhile purple and blue look at one another and wink.

Blue melts within yellow,

Sparkling jollity in a mood that's very mellow.

Sliver whistles at green in delight,

Coloring the golden hues, bright and light.

With springing of the red rose,

A blush kindles in orange blows.

Attired in a rich array,

The glorious white crowns the rainbow tray.

THE EVENING RAIN

Bursting from the clouds, it touches earth's feet.

Washing our sins, it purifies every heart's street.

Turning a dull day into a treat, its rhythm moves each beat.

Playing with the rivers, it dances in the forest.

Swooshing its way through the mountains,

Its pleasant sound soothes the wandering mind

Like the cheerful singing of the chorus.

The chirping birds calm the noise for a while,

I, upon seeing a clear sky, am all smiles.

Upon seeing my naked face, the breeze kisses my candor.

Wishing to hold tranquility forever, I breathe this magic in the air.

The rain is a gem, to be understood in its true light.

Sometimes hidden and sometimes shining,

Untouched and unstrained; it wraps serenity in its arms.

Pure like mirth, I kiss the dew on leaves;

Amidst the storm, till it's shining.

SONOROUS BEAUTY

Pitter-Patter, Burble-Babble,

The gentle rain ripples on my bedroom window.

Whooshing the colorful curtains,

Its joyful drops dance like a flamingo.

Whiff-Whir, Swish-Whizz,

The breezy wind sways my bed cover.

Kissing the soft diary pages,

It flings with the mattress undercover.

Swish-Swash, Whip-Whap,

The beats of my heart swirl in a reverie.

Bursting all emotions,

I follow the shadows of my memory.

ODE TO CREATIVITY

Poetry is the poet's highest form of therapy,

That tells a story of the story.

Confessional poetry releases his hidden emotions,

It helps him to feel lighter.

Poetry glistens plenty a thought of the young philosopher,

Feelings treasured in old chambers are now on paper to decipher.

Words wait eagerly to get dressed in new attire,

Sounds dangle in his heart, giving tune to his desire.

The secret recipe of his magical spree,

Finds its way to diary whenever the poet wishes to flee.

MOMENTS TO SAVOR - A NOTE FOR MY READERS

Having a rough day? Suddenly, you receive a call and the world makes sense again?

No need for words

Smile on face

Big and bright

A cuppa coffee

Makes things right

And your friend sits by your side

XOXO

THANK YOU!

WORD OF THANKS

I would like to thank my parents, Sunita Jain and Sanjay Jain, for teaching me the true meaning of life. For encouraging me not just to own my emotions and feelings but also enlightening me on how to channel my energy and how to put a smile in many a heart.

Special thanks to my best friend Deepak Gahlawat who has seen me openly weep, heard me talk crap, laughed with me, and encouraged me to do what's right. I might have stopped at the first few poems had you not appreciated my work. This book would not have been possible without your support, Deepak.

Sincere thanks to all my readers for joining me in my journey and for staying till the end.

Thank You!

Bibliography

This book includes images which have been leveraged from online sites, such as iStock.

www.ingramcontent.com/pod-product-compliance
Lightning Source LLC
LaVergne TN
LVHW050418160726
843469LV00041B/1135

* 9 7 8 9 3 5 6 1 0 0 2 5 1 *